50 New Zealand Main Courses Recipes for Home

By: Kelly Johnson

Table of Contents

- Roast Lamb with Mint Sauce
- Pavlova with Fresh Berries
- Hangi - Traditional Maori Earth Oven Cooked Feast
- Whitebait Fritters
- Kiwi Burger with Beetroot and Fried Egg
- Mince and Cheese Pie
- Fish and Chips with Lemon Wedges
- Venison Steak with Red Wine Jus
- Crayfish Tail with Garlic Butter
- Bluff Oysters on the Half Shell
- Green Lip Mussel Fritters
- Paua (Abalone) Steaks
- Seafood Chowder with Creamy Base
- Hokey Pokey Ice Cream
- Kina (Sea Urchin) Sushi
- Pork and Puha (Native New Zealand Vegetable) Boil-Up
- Lamb Rack with Rosemary and Garlic
- Hangi Pie - Pie with Hangi Meat and Vegetables
- New Zealand Green Lip Mussels in White Wine Sauce
- Venison Fillet with Blackcurrant Sauce
- Bluff Salmon Fillet with Hollandaise Sauce
- Kingfish Sashimi with Soy Sauce and Wasabi
- Hapuka (Groper) Fillet with Lemon Butter
- Blue Cod Fillet with Macadamia Crust
- Crayfish Risotto with Saffron
- Rewena Bread - Traditional Maori Bread
- New Zealand Meat Pie with Tomato Sauce
- Kumara (Sweet Potato) and Bacon Frittata
- Taro Chips with Aioli
- Manuka Honey Glazed Ham
- Boil-Up - Traditional Maori Stew
- Muttonbird Pie
- Cervena (Farm-raised Venison) Steak with Red Wine Reduction
- Hangi Pizza - Pizza with Hangi Meat and Vegetables
- King Salmon Fillet with Lemon Dill Sauce

- New Zealand Sausages with Onion Gravy
- Blue Cod and Paua (Abalone) Pie
- Mussel Fritter Wrap with Lettuce and Tartare Sauce
- New Zealand Mince Pie with Tomato Sauce
- Tuatua (Native New Zealand Clam) Soup
- New Zealand Lamb Shanks with Rosemary and Garlic
- Whitebait Omelette with Chives
- Taro Fries with Sweet Chili Sauce
- Kingfish Fillet with Mango Salsa
- Kiwi Roast Chicken with Stuffing
- New Zealand Green Lip Mussels in Garlic Butter Sauce
- Crumbed Blue Cod Fillet with Tartare Sauce
- Venison Sausages with Onion Gravy and Mashed Potatoes
- Bluff Oyster Omelette
- Manuka Honey Glazed Duck Breast

Roast Lamb with Mint Sauce

Ingredients:

- 1 leg of lamb (about 4-5 pounds)
- 4 cloves of garlic, minced
- 2 tablespoons fresh rosemary leaves, chopped
- 2 tablespoons fresh thyme leaves, chopped
- 2 tablespoons olive oil
- Salt and pepper to taste
- Mint Sauce:
    - 1 cup fresh mint leaves, finely chopped
    - 1/4 cup boiling water
    - 2 tablespoons sugar
    - 1/4 cup white vinegar

Instructions:

1. Preheat your oven to 375°F (190°C).
2. In a small bowl, mix together the minced garlic, chopped rosemary, chopped thyme, olive oil, salt, and pepper to create a marinade.
3. Place the leg of lamb in a roasting pan and rub the marinade all over the lamb, ensuring it's evenly coated.
4. Roast the lamb in the preheated oven for about 20 minutes per pound for medium-rare doneness. Adjust the cooking time according to your preference for doneness.
5. While the lamb is roasting, prepare the mint sauce. In a heatproof bowl, combine the chopped mint leaves and sugar.
6. Pour the boiling water over the mint leaves and sugar, stirring until the sugar is dissolved.
7. Stir in the white vinegar and let the mint sauce cool to room temperature. Then, refrigerate until ready to serve.
8. Once the lamb is cooked to your desired level of doneness, remove it from the oven and let it rest for about 10-15 minutes before carving.
9. Slice the lamb and serve it with the mint sauce on the side.
10. Enjoy your delicious Roast Lamb with Mint Sauce, a quintessential New Zealand dish that's perfect for special occasions or Sunday dinners!

This dish captures the essence of New Zealand cuisine with its tender, flavorful roast lamb paired with the bright and refreshing mint sauce. It's a timeless favorite that's sure to impress your family and friends!

Pavlova with Fresh Berries

Ingredients:

- 4 large egg whites, at room temperature
- 1 cup granulated sugar
- 1 teaspoon cornstarch
- 1 teaspoon white vinegar
- 1 teaspoon vanilla extract
- 1 cup heavy cream
- 2 tablespoons powdered sugar
- Assorted fresh berries (such as strawberries, blueberries, raspberries, and blackberries)
- Mint leaves for garnish (optional)

Instructions:

1. Preheat your oven to 300°F (150°C). Line a baking sheet with parchment paper.
2. In a clean, dry mixing bowl, beat the egg whites with an electric mixer on medium speed until soft peaks form.
3. Gradually add the granulated sugar, a tablespoon at a time, while continuing to beat the egg whites. Increase the mixer speed to high and beat until stiff peaks form and the meringue is glossy.
4. Sprinkle the cornstarch, white vinegar, and vanilla extract over the meringue. Gently fold them in using a spatula until fully incorporated.
5. Spoon the meringue mixture onto the prepared baking sheet, forming a round mound or nest shape, with slightly raised edges and a shallow well in the center.
6. Place the baking sheet in the preheated oven and immediately reduce the temperature to 250°F (120°C). Bake for 1 hour and 15 minutes to 1 hour and 30 minutes, or until the pavlova is crisp and dry on the outside but still soft and marshmallow-like on the inside.
7. Turn off the oven and leave the pavlova inside to cool completely with the oven door slightly ajar.
8. Once the pavlova is completely cooled, whip the heavy cream and powdered sugar together until stiff peaks form.
9. Spoon the whipped cream into the center of the pavlova, spreading it out evenly.
10. Arrange the fresh berries on top of the whipped cream.
11. Garnish with mint leaves, if desired.

12. Serve the Pavlova with Fresh Berries immediately, and enjoy this delightful and elegant dessert!

This Pavlova with Fresh Berries is a show-stopping dessert that's perfect for special occasions or gatherings. Its light and airy texture, paired with the sweetness of the meringue and the freshness of the berries, creates a harmonious and delightful flavor experience that will impress your guests!

Hangi - Traditional Maori Earth Oven Cooked Feast

Ingredients:

- Meat (such as lamb, pork, chicken, or beef)
- Root vegetables (such as potatoes, kumara/sweet potatoes, and pumpkin)
- Additional vegetables (such as cabbage, carrots, and onions)
- Salt
- Water
- Large banana leaves or aluminum foil
- Rocks or bricks

Instructions:

1. Dig a pit: Choose a spot outdoors where you can dig a pit. The pit should be large enough to fit all your food and deep enough to accommodate a layer of hot rocks or bricks.
2. Heat rocks: Collect medium-sized rocks and heat them in a fire until they are extremely hot. This process can take several hours. Make sure the rocks are heated evenly and thoroughly.
3. Prepare the food: Season the meat and vegetables with salt according to your taste preferences. You can also marinate the meat if desired.
4. Line the pit: Line the bottom of the pit with banana leaves or aluminum foil. This will help prevent the food from burning and add flavor.
5. Place the rocks: Once the rocks are hot, carefully transfer them to the bottom of the pit using tongs or a shovel. Arrange them in a single layer to create a hot stone base.
6. Layer the food: Arrange the seasoned meat and vegetables on top of the hot rocks in the pit. Place the heavier items, such as the meat and root vegetables, closer to the bottom, with lighter items on top.
7. Cover the food: Cover the food with more banana leaves or aluminum foil to trap the steam and heat. Make sure the pit is tightly sealed to prevent steam from escaping.
8. Cook the hangi: Carefully cover the pit with dirt or sand to create an airtight seal. This will help retain the heat and steam while the food cooks. Let the hangi cook for several hours, typically 3 to 4 hours depending on the size of the pit and the amount of food.
9. Uncover and serve: After the cooking time has elapsed, carefully remove the dirt or sand covering the pit. Use caution as steam and heat will escape. Remove the

      banana leaves or aluminum foil covering the food and transfer the cooked meat and vegetables to serving dishes.
10. Enjoy the hangi: Serve the traditional Maori hangi feast with accompaniments such as stuffing, gravy, and sauces. Enjoy the delicious flavors of the tender, smoky meat and perfectly cooked vegetables with friends and family.

Remember that making a traditional hangi is a communal activity often done with family and friends, and it's a great way to celebrate special occasions and cultural heritage.

Whitebait Fritters

Ingredients:

- 1 cup whitebait
- 2 eggs
- 2 tablespoons flour
- Salt and pepper to taste
- Butter or oil for frying

Instructions:

1. Start by rinsing the whitebait under cold water and patting them dry with paper towels. Be gentle to avoid breaking them apart.
2. In a mixing bowl, beat the eggs lightly.
3. Add the flour to the beaten eggs and mix until well combined. The mixture should be thick but still pourable.
4. Gently fold in the whitebait until they are evenly coated with the egg and flour mixture. Season with salt and pepper to taste.
5. Heat a frying pan over medium heat and add a knob of butter or a drizzle of oil.
6. Once the butter is melted or the oil is hot, carefully spoon the whitebait mixture into the pan to form small fritters. You can make them as big or small as you like, but traditionally they are small, bite-sized fritters.
7. Cook the fritters for 1-2 minutes on each side, or until they are golden brown and crispy.
8. Once cooked, remove the fritters from the pan and drain them on paper towels to remove any excess oil.
9. Serve the whitebait fritters hot, with a squeeze of lemon juice and perhaps a dollop of tartare sauce or aioli on the side for dipping.

Enjoy these delicate and delicious fritters as a snack, appetizer, or light meal!

Kiwi Burger with Beetroot and Fried Egg

Ingredients:

- Burger buns
- Ground beef patties (or your choice of protein)
- Sliced beetroot (cooked or canned)
- Fried eggs
- Lettuce leaves
- Tomato slices
- Onion slices
- Cheese slices (optional)
- Tomato sauce (ketchup) or your favorite burger sauce
- Mayonnaise
- Butter or oil for frying

Instructions:

1. Start by cooking your beef patties. Season them with salt and pepper and cook them in a skillet or on a grill until they are cooked to your desired level of doneness. If you're using other proteins like chicken or vegetarian patties, cook them according to their specific instructions.
2. While the patties are cooking, prepare your other burger ingredients. Wash and dry the lettuce leaves, slice the tomatoes and onions, and set them aside.
3. If you're using canned beetroot, drain the slices and pat them dry with paper towels.
4. In a separate skillet, fry your eggs sunny-side up or according to your preference. Make sure the egg yolks are still runny for that delicious, gooey burger experience.
5. Once everything is cooked, toast your burger buns lightly in a toaster or on a skillet with a little butter.
6. Assemble your burgers by spreading mayonnaise on the bottom half of each bun. Then, layer on the lettuce leaves, tomato slices, onion slices, and beetroot slices.
7. Place the cooked beef patties on top of the beetroot slices. If you're using cheese, place a slice on top of each patty so it melts slightly from the heat.
8. Carefully place a fried egg on top of each burger patty.
9. Spread tomato sauce or your favorite burger sauce on the top half of each bun, then place it on top of the egg to complete the burger.

10. Serve your Kiwi Burgers immediately, and enjoy the delicious combination of flavors and textures!

Feel free to customize your Kiwi Burger with additional toppings or condiments to suit your taste preferences. Enjoy!

Mince and Cheese Pie

Ingredients:

For the filling:

- 500g (about 1 lb) beef mince (ground beef)
- 1 onion, finely chopped
- 2 cloves garlic, minced
- 1 carrot, grated
- 1 tablespoon tomato paste
- 1 tablespoon Worcestershire sauce
- 1 teaspoon dried mixed herbs (such as oregano, thyme, rosemary)
- Salt and pepper to taste
- 1 cup grated cheese (cheddar or your preferred cheese)

For the pastry:

- Store-bought shortcrust pastry (enough for a pie base and lid), or you can make your own pastry

For glazing:

- 1 egg, beaten

Instructions:

1. Preheat your oven to 180°C (350°F).
2. In a large frying pan or skillet, heat a little oil over medium heat. Add the chopped onion and minced garlic and cook until softened.
3. Add the beef mince to the pan and cook until browned, breaking it up with a spoon as it cooks.
4. Once the mince is browned, add the grated carrot, tomato paste, Worcestershire sauce, dried herbs, salt, and pepper. Stir well to combine.
5. Allow the mixture to simmer for about 10-15 minutes, or until the flavors have melded together and the mixture has thickened slightly. Taste and adjust seasoning if necessary.

6. Remove the pan from the heat and let the mixture cool slightly.
7. Roll out the shortcrust pastry on a lightly floured surface to fit your pie dish. Line the pie dish with the pastry, leaving some overhang.
8. Spoon the cooled mince mixture into the pastry-lined pie dish, spreading it out evenly.
9. Sprinkle the grated cheese evenly over the top of the mince mixture.
10. Roll out the remaining pastry to create a lid for the pie. Place the lid over the filling and crimp the edges to seal. Trim off any excess pastry.
11. Use a sharp knife to make a few small slits in the top of the pie to allow steam to escape during baking.
12. Brush the top of the pie with beaten egg to create a golden finish when baked.
13. Place the pie in the preheated oven and bake for 30-35 minutes, or until the pastry is golden brown and cooked through.
14. Once baked, remove the pie from the oven and let it cool for a few minutes before slicing and serving.

Enjoy your homemade mince and cheese pie as a delicious and comforting meal or snack!

Fish and Chips with Lemon Wedges

Ingredients:

For the fish:

- White fish fillets (such as cod, haddock, or pollock)
- All-purpose flour, for dredging
- Salt and pepper to taste
- Oil for frying (such as vegetable oil or peanut oil)

For the chips (French fries):

- Potatoes, peeled and cut into thick strips
- Oil for frying
- Salt to taste

For serving:

- Lemon wedges
- Tartar sauce or malt vinegar (optional)

Instructions:

1. Start by preparing the fish. Rinse the fish fillets under cold water and pat them dry with paper towels. Season both sides of the fish fillets with salt and pepper.
2. Dredge each fish fillet in flour, shaking off any excess.
3. Heat oil in a deep fryer or a large skillet over medium-high heat. The oil should be hot enough to fry the fish but not smoking.
4. Carefully place the fish fillets in the hot oil, working in batches if necessary to avoid overcrowding the pan. Fry the fish for 3-5 minutes on each side, or until golden brown and cooked through. The exact cooking time will depend on the thickness of the fish fillets.
5. While the fish is frying, prepare the chips (French fries). Heat oil in a separate deep fryer or skillet over medium-high heat. Fry the potato strips in batches until golden brown and crispy, about 5-7 minutes per batch. Remove the fries from the oil and drain them on paper towels. Sprinkle with salt to taste.
6. Once the fish and chips are cooked, remove them from the oil and drain them on paper towels to remove any excess oil.
7. Serve the fish and chips hot, accompanied by lemon wedges for squeezing over the fish. You can also serve them with tartar sauce or malt vinegar on the side for dipping.

Enjoy this classic fish and chips dish as a delicious and satisfying meal!

Venison Steak with Red Wine Jus

Ingredients:

For the venison steak:

- Venison steaks (about 6-8 ounces each)
- Salt and freshly ground black pepper
- Olive oil or butter for cooking

For the red wine jus:

- 1 cup red wine (such as Merlot, Cabernet Sauvignon, or Pinot Noir)
- 1 shallot, finely chopped
- 1 garlic clove, minced
- 1 tablespoon butter
- 1 cup beef or venison stock (homemade or store-bought)
- Salt and freshly ground black pepper to taste
- Fresh thyme or rosemary sprigs for garnish (optional)

Instructions:

1. Start by seasoning the venison steaks generously with salt and freshly ground black pepper on both sides. Let them sit at room temperature for about 20-30 minutes to allow the meat to absorb the seasoning.
2. While the steaks are resting, prepare the red wine jus. In a saucepan, melt the butter over medium heat. Add the chopped shallot and minced garlic, and sauté until softened and fragrant, about 2-3 minutes.
3. Pour in the red wine and bring it to a simmer. Allow the wine to reduce by about half, stirring occasionally, for about 5-7 minutes.
4. Once the wine has reduced, add the beef or venison stock to the saucepan. Bring the mixture back to a simmer and let it cook for another 5-7 minutes, or until the sauce has thickened slightly.
5. Season the red wine jus with salt and freshly ground black pepper to taste. If desired, strain the sauce through a fine mesh sieve to remove the shallot and garlic pieces. Keep the sauce warm while you cook the venison steaks.
6. Heat a skillet or frying pan over medium-high heat. Add a drizzle of olive oil or a knob of butter to the pan.

7. Once the skillet is hot, carefully add the seasoned venison steaks. Cook the steaks for 3-4 minutes on each side for medium-rare, or adjust the cooking time according to your desired level of doneness.
8. Once the steaks are cooked to your liking, transfer them to a plate and let them rest for a few minutes before serving.
9. To serve, spoon the red wine jus over the venison steaks. Garnish with fresh thyme or rosemary sprigs if desired.

Enjoy your venison steak with red wine jus as a luxurious and flavorful meal!

Crayfish Tail with Garlic Butter

Ingredients:

- Crayfish tails, cooked and shelled
- 4 tablespoons unsalted butter, softened
- 2-3 cloves garlic, minced
- 1 tablespoon fresh parsley, finely chopped
- Salt and freshly ground black pepper to taste
- Lemon wedges for serving
- Optional: crusty bread or rice for serving

Instructions:

1. Start by preparing the garlic butter. In a small bowl, combine the softened butter, minced garlic, chopped parsley, salt, and freshly ground black pepper. Mix well until all the ingredients are evenly incorporated.
2. Preheat your grill or broiler to medium-high heat.
3. Arrange the crayfish tails on a baking sheet or in a grill basket, shell side down.
4. Spoon a generous amount of the garlic butter mixture over each crayfish tail, spreading it evenly.
5. Place the baking sheet or grill basket under the preheated grill or broiler. Cook the crayfish tails for 3-4 minutes, or until the butter is bubbling and the tails are heated through.
6. Carefully remove the crayfish tails from the grill or broiler and transfer them to a serving platter.
7. Serve the crayfish tails immediately, garnished with lemon wedges on the side for squeezing over the tails.
8. You can serve the crayfish tails as an appetizer, alongside crusty bread to soak up the garlic butter, or as a main dish with rice and a side of vegetables.

Enjoy your crayfish tails with garlic butter as a decadent and flavorful seafood treat!

Bluff Oysters on the Half Shell

Ingredients:

- Fresh Bluff oysters (as many as desired)
- Lemon wedges
- Tabasco sauce or your preferred hot sauce (optional)
- Shallot vinegar or mignonette sauce (optional)

Instructions:

1. Start by purchasing fresh Bluff oysters from a reputable seafood market. Make sure they are still alive and tightly closed. It's best to consume them as soon as possible after purchasing for the freshest flavor.
2. Once you're ready to serve the oysters, carefully scrub the shells under cold running water to remove any dirt or debris.
3. Using an oyster knife or a small, sturdy knife, carefully pry open the oyster shells. Slide the knife along the hinge of the shell until it pops open. Be cautious to avoid injuring yourself, and try to keep the oyster liquor (the natural juices inside the shell) intact.
4. Once the oysters are opened, place them on a bed of crushed ice or rock salt to keep them chilled.
5. Serve the Bluff oysters on the half shell with lemon wedges on the side for squeezing over the oysters. This adds a refreshing citrus flavor that complements the brininess of the oysters.
6. Optionally, you can provide Tabasco sauce or your preferred hot sauce for those who enjoy a bit of heat with their oysters.
7. Another optional accompaniment is shallot vinegar or mignonette sauce, which adds a tangy and slightly sweet flavor to the oysters.
8. Encourage your guests to enjoy the Bluff oysters by slurping them directly from the shell, savoring the unique flavor and texture with each bite.
9. Remember to discard any empty shells and provide a bowl for guests to dispose of them.

Enjoy the exquisite taste of Bluff oysters on the half shell as a luxurious and indulgent seafood treat!

Green Lip Mussel Fritters

Ingredients:

- 500g fresh green lip mussels, cleaned and debearded
- 1 cup all-purpose flour
- 1 teaspoon baking powder
- 2 eggs
- 1/4 cup milk
- 2 tablespoons chopped fresh parsley
- Salt and pepper to taste
- Oil for frying (such as vegetable oil or canola oil)
- Lemon wedges for serving

Instructions:

1. Steam the green lip mussels until they open, about 5-7 minutes. Remove them from the shells and chop them into small pieces. Discard any unopened mussels.
2. In a mixing bowl, sift together the flour and baking powder. Add the chopped mussels and parsley, and season with salt and pepper.
3. In a separate bowl, beat the eggs and milk together. Pour the egg mixture into the dry ingredients and stir until well combined. The batter should be thick but still pourable. If it's too thick, you can add a little more milk.
4. Heat oil in a frying pan over medium heat. Spoon the batter into the pan to form fritters, using about 2 tablespoons of batter for each fritter. Flatten them slightly with the back of the spoon.
5. Fry the fritters for 2-3 minutes on each side, or until golden brown and cooked through.
6. Remove the fritters from the pan and drain them on paper towels to remove excess oil.
7. Serve the green lip mussel fritters hot with lemon wedges on the side for squeezing over the top. Enjoy!

These fritters are perfect as an appetizer or a main dish, and they're sure to be a hit with seafood lovers!

Paua (Abalone) Steaks

Ingredients:

- 4 paua (abalone) steaks
- 2 tablespoons butter
- 2 cloves garlic, minced
- 1 tablespoon lemon juice
- Salt and pepper to taste
- Fresh herbs for garnish (optional)

Instructions:

1. Tenderize the paua steaks by pounding them gently with a meat mallet or the back of a heavy spoon. This helps to tenderize the meat and break down any toughness.
2. Heat the butter in a large skillet over medium-high heat. Add the minced garlic and sauté for 1-2 minutes, until fragrant.
3. Place the paua steaks in the skillet in a single layer. Cook them for 1-2 minutes on each side, until they are just cooked through. Be careful not to overcook them, as abalone can become tough and rubbery if cooked for too long.
4. Sprinkle the cooked paua steaks with lemon juice, salt, and pepper to taste.
5. Transfer the paua steaks to serving plates and garnish with fresh herbs, if desired.
6. Serve the paua steaks immediately while they are still hot. They pair well with rice, steamed vegetables, or a fresh salad.

Enjoy these paua steaks as a luxurious seafood dish that's sure to impress!

Seafood Chowder with Creamy Base

Ingredients:

- 500g mixed seafood (such as shrimp, scallops, white fish, and/or mussels), peeled and deveined if necessary
- 3 tablespoons butter
- 1 onion, diced
- 2 cloves garlic, minced
- 2 stalks celery, diced
- 2 carrots, diced
- 2 potatoes, peeled and diced
- 4 cups seafood or fish stock
- 1 cup heavy cream
- 1/4 cup all-purpose flour
- 1 bay leaf
- 1 teaspoon dried thyme
- Salt and pepper to taste
- Chopped fresh parsley for garnish

Instructions:

1. In a large pot or Dutch oven, melt the butter over medium heat. Add the diced onion, garlic, celery, and carrots. Cook for 5-7 minutes, until the vegetables are softened.
2. Stir in the flour and cook for an additional 2 minutes, stirring constantly, to create a roux.
3. Gradually pour in the seafood or fish stock, stirring constantly to prevent lumps from forming. Add the bay leaf and dried thyme.
4. Bring the chowder to a simmer, then add the diced potatoes. Cook for 10-12 minutes, or until the potatoes are tender.
5. Stir in the mixed seafood and cook for an additional 3-5 minutes, until the seafood is cooked through.
6. Reduce the heat to low and pour in the heavy cream. Stir gently to combine.
7. Season the chowder with salt and pepper to taste. Remove the bay leaf.
8. Ladle the seafood chowder into bowls and garnish with chopped fresh parsley.
9. Serve the chowder hot, with crusty bread or oyster crackers on the side.

Enjoy this creamy and flavorful seafood chowder as a comforting meal on a chilly day!

Hokey Pokey Ice Cream

Ingredients:

For the Hokey Pokey (Honeycomb Toffee):

- 1 cup granulated sugar
- 4 tablespoons golden syrup or corn syrup
- 1 1/2 teaspoons baking soda

For the Ice Cream Base:

- 2 cups heavy cream
- 1 cup whole milk
- 3/4 cup granulated sugar
- Pinch of salt
- 1 vanilla bean pod, split lengthwise (or 2 teaspoons vanilla extract)
- 5 large egg yolks

Instructions:

1. Prepare the Hokey Pokey (Honeycomb Toffee):
    - Line a baking sheet with parchment paper and set aside.
    - In a medium saucepan, combine the sugar and golden syrup (or corn syrup) over medium heat. Stir until the sugar dissolves.
    - Once the mixture starts to boil, stop stirring and let it cook until it reaches a deep golden caramel color, about 5-7 minutes. Be careful not to let it burn.
    - Remove the saucepan from the heat and quickly whisk in the baking soda. The mixture will bubble up vigorously.
    - Immediately pour the hot mixture onto the prepared baking sheet. Let it cool and harden completely, then break it into small pieces. Set aside.
2. Prepare the Ice Cream Base:
    - In a saucepan, combine the heavy cream, whole milk, half of the sugar, and salt. If using a vanilla bean pod, scrape the seeds into the mixture and add the pod as well. Heat the mixture over medium heat until it just begins to simmer. Remove from heat and let steep for 30 minutes.

- In a separate bowl, whisk together the egg yolks and the remaining sugar until pale and slightly thickened.
- Gradually pour the warm cream mixture into the egg yolk mixture, whisking constantly to temper the eggs.
- Return the mixture to the saucepan and cook over low heat, stirring constantly, until it thickens and coats the back of a spoon (about 170°F or 77°C). Do not let it boil.
- Strain the custard through a fine-mesh sieve into a clean bowl. If using vanilla extract, stir it in now.
- Cover the bowl with plastic wrap, pressing it directly onto the surface of the custard to prevent a skin from forming. Chill the custard in the refrigerator until completely cold, preferably overnight.

3. Churn the Ice Cream:
   - Once the custard is cold, churn it in an ice cream maker according to the manufacturer's instructions.
   - During the last few minutes of churning, add the broken pieces of Hokey Pokey (honeycomb toffee) to the ice cream and churn until evenly distributed.
   - Transfer the churned ice cream to a freezer-safe container and freeze until firm, at least 4 hours or overnight.
4. Serve:
   - Scoop the Hokey Pokey ice cream into bowls or cones and enjoy!

This homemade Hokey Pokey ice cream is a delightful treat with its creamy texture and sweet, crunchy bits of honeycomb toffee scattered throughout.

Kina (Sea Urchin) Sushi

Ingredients:

- Fresh kina (sea urchin) roe
- Sushi rice (prepared according to your favorite recipe)
- Nori sheets (seaweed), cut into strips (optional)
- Soy sauce, for dipping
- Wasabi paste, for serving (optional)
- Pickled ginger, for serving (optional)

Instructions:

1. Prepare the sushi rice according to your favorite recipe. Let it cool to room temperature.
2. Gently open the kina shells to reveal the roe inside. Carefully remove the roe from the shells and place them in a small bowl. Discard the shells.
3. If using nori sheets, cut them into strips that are slightly narrower than the width of your sushi rolls.
4. Take a small amount of sushi rice and form it into a small oblong shape, about the size of your index finger.
5. Place a small spoonful of kina roe on top of the rice, gently pressing it down to adhere.
6. If using nori strips, wrap them around the sushi rice and kina, securing them with a dab of water if necessary.
7. Repeat the process to make additional kina sushi rolls.
8. Serve the kina sushi with soy sauce for dipping. If desired, serve with wasabi paste and pickled ginger on the side.
9. Enjoy your homemade kina sushi as a delicious and exotic treat!

Note: When handling kina roe, it's important to handle it gently to avoid breaking the delicate membranes. Additionally, kina sushi is best enjoyed fresh, so prepare and serve it soon after assembling.

Pork and Puha (Native New Zealand Vegetable) Boil-Up

Ingredients:

- 500g pork shoulder or belly, diced into bite-sized pieces
- 1 onion, diced
- 2 cloves garlic, minced
- 2-3 cups chopped puha leaves (sow thistle), washed thoroughly
- 2-3 cups chopped watercress or spinach (substitute for puha if unavailable)
- 2-3 potatoes, peeled and diced
- 2-3 carrots, peeled and diced
- Salt and pepper to taste
- Optional: 1-2 kumara (sweet potatoes), peeled and diced
- Optional: 1-2 cups chopped pumpkin or squash
- Optional: 1-2 cups chopped cabbage
- Optional: 1-2 cups chopped celery
- Water or broth, enough to cover the ingredients
- Optional: Kumara bread or bread rolls, for serving

Instructions:

1. In a large pot or Dutch oven, heat a small amount of oil over medium heat. Add the diced pork and cook until browned on all sides.
2. Add the diced onion and minced garlic to the pot. Cook until the onion is translucent and fragrant.
3. Add enough water or broth to cover the pork and vegetables. Bring the mixture to a simmer.
4. Add the diced potatoes, carrots, and any optional vegetables you're using (such as kumara, pumpkin, cabbage, or celery). Season with salt and pepper to taste.
5. Simmer the boil-up for about 30-40 minutes, or until the pork and vegetables are tender. Skim off any foam or impurities that rise to the surface during cooking.
6. Add the chopped puha leaves and watercress (or spinach) to the pot. Simmer for an additional 5-10 minutes, until the greens are wilted and tender.
7. Taste the broth and adjust the seasoning if necessary.
8. Serve the pork and puha boil-up hot, ladled into bowls. Enjoy with kumara bread or bread rolls on the side.

This hearty and nourishing dish is a comforting meal, perfect for cooler days. It's also a great way to enjoy the unique flavor of puha and other New Zealand vegetables.

Lamb Rack with Rosemary and Garlic

Ingredients:

- 2 racks of lamb, about 8 ribs each
- 4 cloves of garlic, minced
- 2 tablespoons fresh rosemary leaves, chopped
- 2 tablespoons olive oil
- Salt and pepper, to taste

Instructions:

1. Preheat your oven to 400°F (200°C).
2. In a small bowl, mix together the minced garlic, chopped rosemary, olive oil, salt, and pepper to create a marinade.
3. Place the racks of lamb on a cutting board and pat them dry with paper towels. This will help the marinade to adhere better.
4. Rub the marinade all over the racks of lamb, making sure to coat them evenly on all sides.
5. Heat a large oven-proof skillet over medium-high heat. Once hot, add a bit of olive oil to the skillet.
6. Sear the racks of lamb in the skillet for about 2-3 minutes on each side, until they are nicely browned.
7. Transfer the skillet to the preheated oven and roast the lamb racks for about 15-20 minutes for medium-rare, or longer if you prefer your lamb more well-done. Use a meat thermometer to check for doneness – the internal temperature should reach 145°F (63°C) for medium-rare or 160°F (71°C) for medium.
8. Once cooked to your desired doneness, remove the skillet from the oven and let the lamb racks rest for a few minutes before slicing.
9. To serve, slice the racks of lamb between the bones into individual chops. Arrange them on a serving platter and garnish with additional fresh rosemary sprigs, if desired.
10. Serve the lamb racks with your favorite sides, such as roasted potatoes, steamed vegetables, or a fresh salad.

Enjoy your beautifully seasoned and perfectly cooked lamb racks with rosemary and garlic!

Hangi Pie - Pie with Hangi Meat and Vegetables

Ingredients:

For the Filling:

- Leftover hangi meat (such as lamb, pork, or chicken), shredded or diced
- Leftover hangi vegetables (such as kumara, potato, pumpkin, and carrot), diced
- Gravy or sauce of your choice (optional)

For the Pastry:

- 2 cups all-purpose flour
- 1/2 teaspoon salt
- 2/3 cup cold butter, diced
- 4-6 tablespoons ice water

Instructions:

1. Preheat your oven to 400°F (200°C).
2. Prepare the filling by mixing together the shredded or diced hangi meat and vegetables in a bowl. If desired, add gravy or sauce to moisten the filling and enhance the flavor.
3. In a large mixing bowl, combine the flour and salt. Add the diced butter and use your fingertips or a pastry cutter to rub the butter into the flour until the mixture resembles coarse crumbs.
4. Gradually add the ice water, 1 tablespoon at a time, and mix until the dough comes together into a ball. Be careful not to overwork the dough.
5. Divide the dough into two equal portions. Roll out one portion of the dough on a lightly floured surface to fit the base of a pie dish.
6. Transfer the rolled-out pastry to the pie dish and press it gently into the bottom and sides. Trim any excess pastry hanging over the edges.
7. Spoon the hangi meat and vegetable filling into the pastry-lined pie dish, spreading it out evenly.
8. Roll out the remaining portion of the dough and place it over the filling. Press the edges of the top and bottom crusts together to seal the pie.

9. Use a sharp knife to make a few small slits in the top crust to allow steam to escape during baking.
10. Optional: Brush the top crust with beaten egg for a golden finish.
11. Place the pie in the preheated oven and bake for 25-30 minutes, or until the pastry is golden brown and crispy.
12. Remove the hangi pie from the oven and let it cool for a few minutes before slicing and serving.

Enjoy your delicious hangi pie, filled with the flavors of traditional hangi meat and vegetables, encased in a flaky pastry crust!

New Zealand Green Lip Mussels in White Wine Sauce

Ingredients:

- 1 kg fresh New Zealand green lip mussels, cleaned and debearded
- 2 tablespoons butter
- 2 cloves garlic, minced
- 1 shallot, finely chopped
- 1 cup dry white wine (such as Sauvignon Blanc)
- 1/2 cup heavy cream
- 1 tablespoon fresh lemon juice
- 2 tablespoons chopped fresh parsley
- Salt and pepper to taste
- Crusty bread or French baguette, for serving

Instructions:

1. In a large skillet or pot, melt the butter over medium heat. Add the minced garlic and chopped shallot, and sauté for 1-2 minutes until fragrant.
2. Pour the white wine into the skillet and bring it to a simmer. Let it cook for 2-3 minutes to reduce slightly.
3. Add the cleaned and debearded green lip mussels to the skillet. Cover with a lid and steam the mussels for 5-7 minutes, or until they have opened. Discard any mussels that do not open.
4. Remove the cooked mussels from the skillet using a slotted spoon and transfer them to a serving bowl. Cover to keep warm.
5. To the remaining liquid in the skillet, add the heavy cream and fresh lemon juice. Stir to combine and let the sauce simmer for another 2-3 minutes until slightly thickened.
6. Season the sauce with salt and pepper to taste. Stir in the chopped fresh parsley.
7. Pour the white wine sauce over the cooked green lip mussels in the serving bowl.
8. Serve the New Zealand green lip mussels in white wine sauce immediately, accompanied by crusty bread or French baguette slices for dipping into the flavorful sauce.

Enjoy this delicious seafood dish as an appetizer or main course, perfect for a special occasion or a cozy dinner at home!

Venison Fillet with Blackcurrant Sauce

Ingredients:

For the Venison Fillet:

- 4 venison fillets (about 6-8 ounces each)
- Salt and pepper to taste
- 2 tablespoons olive oil
- 2 cloves garlic, minced
- 2 sprigs fresh rosemary

For the Blackcurrant Sauce:

- 1 cup blackcurrants (fresh or frozen)
- 1/2 cup red wine
- 1/4 cup beef or venison stock
- 2 tablespoons balsamic vinegar
- 2 tablespoons honey or maple syrup
- 1 tablespoon butter
- Salt and pepper to taste

Instructions:

1. Season the venison fillets generously with salt and pepper on both sides.
2. Heat the olive oil in a large skillet over medium-high heat. Add the minced garlic and fresh rosemary sprigs to the skillet and cook for 1-2 minutes until fragrant.
3. Add the venison fillets to the skillet and sear them for 2-3 minutes on each side, or until they are browned on the outside but still pink in the center (for medium-rare). Adjust cooking time according to your desired level of doneness. Remove the venison fillets from the skillet and let them rest on a plate while you prepare the sauce.
4. In the same skillet, add the blackcurrants, red wine, beef or venison stock, balsamic vinegar, and honey or maple syrup. Bring the mixture to a simmer over medium heat.
5. Let the sauce simmer for 8-10 minutes, or until the blackcurrants have softened and the sauce has thickened slightly.

6. Remove the rosemary sprigs from the skillet and discard them. Stir in the butter until melted and incorporated into the sauce. Season the sauce with salt and pepper to taste.
7. Return the venison fillets to the skillet and coat them with the blackcurrant sauce. Let them heat through for 1-2 minutes.
8. Serve the venison fillets with blackcurrant sauce immediately, drizzling extra sauce over the top if desired. Garnish with fresh herbs, such as parsley or thyme, if desired.

Enjoy this elegant and flavorful dish of venison fillet with blackcurrant sauce, perfect for a special dinner occasion!

Bluff Salmon Fillet with Hollandaise Sauce

Ingredients:

For the Salmon Fillet:

- 4 salmon fillets (about 6-8 ounces each), skin-on
- Salt and pepper to taste
- 2 tablespoons olive oil or melted butter
- Lemon wedges, for serving

For the Hollandaise Sauce:

- 3 large egg yolks
- 1 tablespoon lemon juice
- 1/2 cup unsalted butter, melted and hot
- Pinch of cayenne pepper (optional)
- Salt and pepper to taste

Instructions:

1. Preheat your oven to 375°F (190°C).
2. Season the salmon fillets generously with salt and pepper on both sides.
3. Heat the olive oil or melted butter in a large oven-proof skillet over medium-high heat. Once hot, add the salmon fillets to the skillet, skin-side down.
4. Sear the salmon fillets for 2-3 minutes on the skin side until golden brown and crispy. Flip the fillets over and sear for an additional 1-2 minutes on the flesh side.
5. Transfer the skillet to the preheated oven and bake the salmon fillets for 8-10 minutes, or until they are cooked through and flake easily with a fork.
6. While the salmon is baking, prepare the hollandaise sauce. In a heatproof bowl set over a pot of simmering water (double boiler), whisk together the egg yolks and lemon juice until thickened and pale in color.
7. Slowly drizzle the hot melted butter into the egg yolk mixture, whisking constantly, until the sauce is smooth and thickened. Be careful not to add the butter too quickly, as this can cause the sauce to break.

8. Once all the butter has been incorporated, remove the bowl from the heat. Season the hollandaise sauce with a pinch of cayenne pepper (if using), salt, and pepper to taste. Keep the sauce warm until ready to serve.
9. Remove the salmon fillets from the oven and transfer them to serving plates. Drizzle the hollandaise sauce over the top of the salmon fillets.
10. Serve the Bluff salmon fillets with hollandaise sauce immediately, accompanied by lemon wedges on the side for squeezing over the salmon.

Enjoy this decadent and elegant dish of Bluff salmon fillet with creamy hollandaise sauce, perfect for a special dinner occasion!

Kingfish Sashimi with Soy Sauce and Wasabi

Ingredients:

- 200g fresh kingfish fillet, sushi-grade
- Soy sauce, for dipping
- Wasabi paste, for serving
- Pickled ginger, for serving (optional)
- Shiso leaves or thinly sliced green onions, for garnish (optional)
- Sesame seeds, for garnish (optional)

Instructions:

1. Start by ensuring your kingfish fillet is sushi-grade, meaning it's been frozen to kill any potential parasites. Thaw it if necessary and pat it dry with paper towels.
2. Using a sharp knife, slice the kingfish fillet into thin slices. You can slice it against the grain for a more tender texture.
3. Arrange the kingfish slices on a serving platter in a single layer. You can slightly overlap them for a decorative effect.
4. Serve the kingfish sashimi with small dishes of soy sauce and wasabi paste on the side for dipping. You can also add pickled ginger for cleansing the palate between bites.
5. Optionally, garnish the sashimi with shiso leaves, thinly sliced green onions, or sesame seeds for added flavor and visual appeal.
6. Enjoy the kingfish sashimi immediately while it's fresh and flavorful.

Note: Kingfish sashimi is best enjoyed when the fish is very fresh, so be sure to purchase it from a reputable source. Additionally, handle the fish with care and keep it refrigerated until serving to ensure food safety.

Hapuka (Groper) Fillet with Lemon Butter

Ingredients:

- 4 hapuka fillets (about 6-8 ounces each)
- Salt and pepper to taste
- 2 tablespoons olive oil or melted butter
- Lemon wedges, for serving

For the Lemon Butter Sauce:

- 1/4 cup unsalted butter
- 2 tablespoons fresh lemon juice
- 1 tablespoon chopped fresh parsley
- Salt and pepper to taste

Instructions:

1. Season the hapuka fillets generously with salt and pepper on both sides.
2. Heat the olive oil or melted butter in a large skillet over medium-high heat.
3. Once hot, add the hapuka fillets to the skillet. Cook the fillets for 3-4 minutes on each side, or until they are cooked through and opaque in the center. The cooking time will depend on the thickness of the fillets.
4. While the hapuka fillets are cooking, prepare the lemon butter sauce. In a small saucepan, melt the butter over medium heat.
5. Once the butter is melted, add the fresh lemon juice and chopped parsley to the saucepan. Stir to combine.
6. Season the lemon butter sauce with salt and pepper to taste. Keep the sauce warm over low heat until ready to serve.
7. Once the hapuka fillets are cooked, transfer them to serving plates. Drizzle the lemon butter sauce over the top of the fillets.
8. Serve the hapuka fillets with lemon butter sauce immediately, accompanied by lemon wedges on the side for squeezing over the fish.
9. Optionally, garnish the fillets with additional chopped parsley for a pop of color.

Enjoy this delicious and elegant dish of hapuka fillet with lemon butter sauce, perfect for a special dinner occasion!

Blue Cod Fillet with Macadamia Crust

Ingredients:

- 4 blue cod fillets (about 6-8 ounces each)
- Salt and pepper to taste
- 1 cup macadamia nuts, finely chopped or ground
- 1/2 cup panko breadcrumbs
- 2 tablespoons fresh parsley, chopped
- 2 tablespoons olive oil
- Lemon wedges, for serving

Instructions:

1. Preheat your oven to 400°F (200°C). Line a baking sheet with parchment paper or foil and lightly grease it with olive oil.
2. Season the blue cod fillets with salt and pepper on both sides.
3. In a shallow dish, combine the finely chopped or ground macadamia nuts, panko breadcrumbs, and chopped fresh parsley. Mix well to combine.
4. Brush each blue cod fillet lightly with olive oil on both sides.
5. Press each fillet into the macadamia nut mixture, coating both sides evenly with the crust mixture. Press gently to adhere the crust to the fish.
6. Place the coated blue cod fillets on the prepared baking sheet.
7. Bake the blue cod fillets in the preheated oven for 12-15 minutes, or until the fish is cooked through and the crust is golden and crispy.
8. Remove the blue cod fillets from the oven and let them rest for a few minutes before serving.
9. Serve the blue cod fillets with macadamia crust hot, accompanied by lemon wedges on the side for squeezing over the fish.
10. Enjoy this delicious and flavorful dish as a main course, paired with your favorite sides such as roasted vegetables, rice, or a fresh salad.

This blue cod fillet with macadamia crust is sure to impress with its crispy exterior and tender, flaky fish inside. It's perfect for a special dinner occasion or a weeknight treat!

Crayfish Risotto with Saffron

Ingredients:

- 2 cups Arborio rice
- 4 cups seafood or chicken broth
- 2 tablespoons olive oil
- 1 onion, finely chopped
- 2 cloves garlic, minced
- 1 cup dry white wine
- Pinch of saffron threads
- 1 lb crayfish tails, cooked and shelled
- 1/2 cup grated Parmesan cheese
- Salt and pepper to taste
- Fresh parsley, chopped, for garnish (optional)

Instructions:

1. In a small bowl, steep the saffron threads in 1/4 cup of hot water for 10-15 minutes to release their flavor and color.
2. In a large skillet or saucepan, heat the olive oil over medium heat. Add the chopped onion and minced garlic and sauté until softened and translucent, about 3-4 minutes.
3. Add the Arborio rice to the skillet and stir to coat the rice with the oil, onion, and garlic mixture. Toast the rice for 1-2 minutes, stirring constantly.
4. Pour in the dry white wine and stir until it has been absorbed by the rice.
5. Begin adding the seafood or chicken broth to the skillet, one ladleful at a time, stirring frequently and allowing each addition to be absorbed before adding the next. Continue this process until the rice is creamy and tender, but still slightly al dente, about 18-20 minutes.
6. Stir in the steeped saffron threads and their liquid, along with the cooked crayfish tails. Continue to cook for an additional 2-3 minutes, until the crayfish tails are heated through.
7. Remove the skillet from the heat and stir in the grated Parmesan cheese until melted and incorporated into the risotto. Season with salt and pepper to taste.
8. Serve the crayfish risotto with saffron immediately, garnished with chopped fresh parsley if desired.

Enjoy this decadent and flavorful crayfish risotto with saffron as a main course for a special dinner occasion! Pair it with a crisp white wine to complement the dish's flavors.

Rewena Bread - Traditional Maori Bread

Ingredients:

For the Starter (Rewena):

- 2 medium-sized potatoes
- 2 cups warm water
- 2 cups all-purpose flour

For the Bread:

- 4 cups all-purpose flour
- 1 teaspoon salt
- 1/4 cup sugar
- 1/2 teaspoon baking soda
- 1/4 cup warm water

Instructions:

1. Prepare the Starter (Rewena):
    - Peel and chop the potatoes into small pieces. Place them in a large bowl and cover them with the 2 cups of warm water.
    - Let the potatoes soak overnight or for at least 12 hours to allow them to ferment.
    - After fermenting, strain the liquid from the potatoes into a clean bowl, discarding the potato pieces.
    - Add the 2 cups of all-purpose flour to the potato liquid and mix well to form a thick paste. Cover the bowl with a clean cloth and let it sit in a warm place for 2-3 days, stirring occasionally, until it becomes bubbly and sour-smelling.
2. Make the Bread:
    - Preheat your oven to 350°F (175°C). Grease a loaf pan or line it with parchment paper.
    - In a large mixing bowl, sift together the 4 cups of all-purpose flour, salt, and sugar.
    - In a small bowl, dissolve the baking soda in the 1/4 cup of warm water.
    - Add the fermented Rewena starter to the flour mixture, along with the dissolved baking soda. Mix well to combine, forming a dough.

- Turn the dough out onto a lightly floured surface and knead it for 5-10 minutes, until smooth and elastic.
- Shape the dough into a loaf and place it into the prepared loaf pan.
- Bake the bread in the preheated oven for 40-45 minutes, or until it is golden brown and sounds hollow when tapped on the bottom.
- Remove the bread from the oven and let it cool in the pan for 10 minutes before transferring it to a wire rack to cool completely.

3. Serve:
   - Slice the Rewena bread and serve it warm or at room temperature with butter or your favorite spreads.

Enjoy this traditional Māori Rewena bread as a delicious and unique addition to your table!

New Zealand Meat Pie with Tomato Sauce

Ingredients:

For the Meat Filling:

- 500g minced beef or lamb
- 1 onion, finely chopped
- 2 cloves garlic, minced
- 2 tablespoons tomato paste
- 1 tablespoon Worcestershire sauce
- 1 teaspoon dried thyme
- Salt and pepper to taste
- 1 cup beef stock
- 2 tablespoons all-purpose flour (optional, for thickening)

For the Pie Crust:

- 2 sheets of store-bought puff pastry, thawed
- 1 egg, beaten (for egg wash)

For Serving:

- Tomato sauce (ketchup) or HP sauce

Instructions:

1. Preheat your oven to 200°C (400°F). Line a baking sheet with parchment paper.
2. In a large skillet or frying pan, heat some oil over medium heat. Add the chopped onion and minced garlic and cook until softened, about 3-4 minutes.
3. Add the minced beef or lamb to the skillet and cook until browned, breaking it up with a spoon as it cooks.
4. Stir in the tomato paste, Worcestershire sauce, dried thyme, salt, and pepper. Cook for another 2-3 minutes to allow the flavors to meld.
5. If you prefer a thicker filling, sprinkle the flour over the meat mixture and stir to combine. Cook for another minute.

6. Pour in the beef stock and stir well. Allow the mixture to simmer for 10-15 minutes, or until the liquid has reduced and the filling has thickened. Remove from heat and let it cool slightly.
7. While the filling is cooling, prepare the pie crust. Cut each sheet of puff pastry into quarters, creating 8 squares in total.
8. Spoon the cooled meat filling onto one half of each pastry square, leaving a border around the edges.
9. Fold the other half of the pastry over the filling to create a rectangle shape. Press the edges together firmly to seal, then crimp the edges with a fork.
10. Place the assembled pies onto the prepared baking sheet. Brush the tops of the pies with beaten egg for a golden finish.
11. Bake in the preheated oven for 20-25 minutes, or until the pastry is golden brown and crispy.
12. Remove the pies from the oven and let them cool for a few minutes before serving.
13. Serve the New Zealand meat pies with tomato sauce or HP sauce on the side for dipping.

Enjoy these delicious and comforting meat pies, a beloved staple of New Zealand cuisine!

Kumara (Sweet Potato) and Bacon Frittata

Ingredients:

- 1 large kumara (sweet potato), peeled and diced into small cubes
- 6 slices of bacon, chopped
- 1 onion, diced
- 6 eggs
- 1/4 cup milk or cream
- Salt and pepper to taste
- 1 tablespoon olive oil or butter
- 1 cup shredded cheese (such as cheddar or Gruyere)
- Fresh parsley or chives, chopped, for garnish (optional)

Instructions:

1. Preheat your oven to 375°F (190°C).
2. Heat the olive oil or butter in a large oven-proof skillet over medium heat. Add the diced kumara and cook for 5-7 minutes, or until the kumara is tender and lightly browned. Remove from the skillet and set aside.
3. In the same skillet, add the chopped bacon and diced onion. Cook until the bacon is crispy and the onion is softened, about 5-7 minutes. Remove from the skillet and set aside with the cooked kumara.
4. In a large mixing bowl, whisk together the eggs, milk or cream, salt, and pepper until well combined.
5. Return the skillet to the stove over medium heat. Add the cooked kumara, bacon, and onion mixture back to the skillet and spread them out evenly.
6. Pour the egg mixture over the top of the kumara and bacon mixture in the skillet. Gently stir to distribute the ingredients evenly.
7. Sprinkle the shredded cheese over the top of the frittata mixture.
8. Transfer the skillet to the preheated oven and bake for 20-25 minutes, or until the frittata is set in the center and the top is golden brown.
9. Once cooked,

Taro Chips with Aioli

Ingredients:

For the Taro Chips:

- 2 medium-sized taro roots
- Vegetable oil for frying
- Salt to taste

For the Aioli:

- 1/2 cup mayonnaise
- 1 clove garlic, minced
- 1 tablespoon lemon juice
- 1 teaspoon Dijon mustard
- Salt and pepper to taste

Instructions:

1. Peel the taro roots and slice them thinly using a mandoline slicer or a sharp knife. Aim for slices that are about 1/8 inch thick.
2. Rinse the taro slices under cold water to remove excess starch. Pat them dry with paper towels.
3. Heat vegetable oil in a deep fryer or a large pot to 350°F (175°C).
4. Working in batches, carefully fry the taro slices in the hot oil until they are golden brown and crispy, about 3-4 minutes. Use a slotted spoon to transfer the chips to a plate lined with paper towels to drain excess oil.
5. Sprinkle the hot taro chips with salt immediately after frying. Repeat the frying process with the remaining taro slices.
6. To make the aioli, combine the mayonnaise, minced garlic, lemon juice, and Dijon mustard in a bowl. Mix until well combined.
7. Season the aioli with salt and pepper to taste. Adjust the seasoning as needed.
8. Serve the crispy taro chips with the homemade aioli on the side for dipping.

Enjoy your homemade taro chips with aioli as a tasty and satisfying snack or appetizer!

Manuka Honey Glazed Ham

Ingredients:

- 1 bone-in fully cooked ham (about 8-10 pounds)
- 1 cup Manuka honey
- 1/4 cup Dijon mustard
- 1/4 cup brown sugar
- 2 tablespoons apple cider vinegar
- 1 teaspoon ground cloves
- 1/2 teaspoon ground cinnamon
- 1/4 teaspoon ground nutmeg

Instructions:

1. Preheat your oven to 325°F (160°C).
2. Place the ham in a roasting pan, fat side up. Score the surface of the ham with shallow diagonal cuts, making diamond shapes.
3. In a small saucepan, combine the Manuka honey, Dijon mustard, brown sugar, apple cider vinegar, ground cloves, ground cinnamon, and ground nutmeg. Heat the mixture over medium heat, stirring constantly, until the ingredients are well combined and the mixture is smooth.
4. Brush about half of the honey glaze over the surface of the ham, making sure to coat it evenly.
5. Cover the ham loosely with aluminum foil and bake in the preheated oven for about 1 hour and 30 minutes to 2 hours, or until heated through. Baste the ham with the remaining honey glaze every 30 minutes or so.
6. Remove the foil during the last 30 minutes of cooking to allow the surface of the ham to caramelize and become golden brown.
7. Once the ham is heated through and the glaze is caramelized, remove it from the oven and transfer it to a serving platter.
8. Let the ham rest for about 10-15 minutes before slicing and serving.
9. Serve the Manuka honey glazed ham slices with any remaining glaze drizzled over the top.

Enjoy this delicious Manuka honey glazed ham as the centerpiece of your holiday table or special occasion meal!

Boil-Up - Traditional Maori Stew

Ingredients:

- 500g beef or pork bones (or a combination)
- 500g pork belly or pork shoulder, cut into chunks
- 2 onions, peeled and chopped
- 2-3 carrots, peeled and cut into chunks
- 2-3 potatoes, peeled and cut into chunks
- 2-3 kumara (sweet potatoes), peeled and cut into chunks
- 2-3 parsnips, peeled and cut into chunks
- 2-3 pieces of pumpkin, peeled and cut into chunks
- 2-3 cups water or beef broth
- Salt and pepper to taste
- 1 cup self-raising flour
- 1/2 cup water or milk (for dumplings)

Instructions:

1. In a large pot, combine the beef or pork bones, pork belly or pork shoulder, and chopped onions. Cover with water or beef broth and bring to a boil over high heat.
2. Once boiling, reduce the heat to low and let the meat simmer for about 1-2 hours, or until it's tender and falling off the bones.
3. Skim off any foam or impurities that rise to the surface during cooking.
4. Once the meat is tender, add the carrots, potatoes, kumara, parsnips, and pumpkin to the pot. Add more water or broth if needed to cover the vegetables.
5. Season the stew with salt and pepper to taste. Continue to simmer for another 20-30 minutes, or until the vegetables are cooked through and tender.
6. In the meantime, prepare the dumplings. In a bowl, mix together the self-raising flour and water or milk until a soft dough forms. Shape the dough into small balls.
7. Drop the dumplings into the pot of simmering stew. Cover the pot and let the dumplings cook for about 10-15 minutes, or until they are puffed up and cooked through.
8. Once the stew and dumplings are cooked, remove the pot from the heat.
9. Serve the boil-up hot in bowls, making sure to include a mix of meat, vegetables, and dumplings in each serving.

Enjoy this comforting and hearty traditional Māori boil-up with your family and friends!

Muttonbird Pie

Ingredients:

For the Filling:

- 500g muttonbird meat, cleaned and shredded (you may need to order this from specialty suppliers)
- 1 onion, finely chopped
- 2 cloves garlic, minced
- 2 carrots, peeled and diced
- 2 celery stalks, diced
- 2 tablespoons butter or oil
- 2 tablespoons all-purpose flour
- 2 cups chicken or vegetable broth
- Salt and pepper to taste
- 1 tablespoon chopped fresh thyme or rosemary (optional)

For the Pie Crust:

- 2 sheets of store-bought puff pastry, thawed
- 1 egg, beaten (for egg wash)

Instructions:

1. Preheat your oven to 375°F (190°C). Grease a pie dish or baking dish with butter or oil.
2. In a large skillet or frying pan, heat the butter or oil over medium heat. Add the chopped onion and minced garlic, and sauté until softened and fragrant, about 2-3 minutes.
3. Add the diced carrots and celery to the skillet, and cook for another 5 minutes, until the vegetables are softened.
4. Stir in the shredded muttonbird meat and cook for another 5 minutes, until heated through.
5. Sprinkle the flour over the meat and vegetables in the skillet, and stir to coat evenly. Cook for 1-2 minutes to cook off the raw flour taste.
6. Slowly pour in the chicken or vegetable broth, stirring constantly, until the mixture thickens and becomes a gravy-like consistency. Add the chopped fresh thyme or

rosemary, if using. Season with salt and pepper to taste. Remove from heat and let the filling cool slightly.
7. While the filling is cooling, prepare the pie crust. Roll out one sheet of puff pastry and use it to line the bottom of the greased pie dish. Trim any excess pastry hanging over the edges.
8. Pour the cooled muttonbird filling into the pie dish, spreading it out evenly.
9. Roll out the second sheet of puff pastry and place it over the top of the filling. Press the edges of the top and bottom crusts together to seal, then crimp the edges with a fork.
10. Brush the top of the pie with beaten egg for a golden finish.
11. Use a sharp knife to make a few small slits in the top crust to allow steam to escape during baking.
12. Place the pie in the preheated oven and bake for 30-35 minutes, or until the crust is golden brown and crispy.
13. Remove the muttonbird pie from the oven and let it cool for a few minutes before slicing and serving.

Enjoy this unique and flavorful Māori dish of muttonbird pie as a special treat!

Cervena (Farm-raised Venison) Steak with Red Wine Reduction

Ingredients:

For the Cervena Steak:

- 4 Cervena venison steaks (about 6-8 ounces each)
- Salt and pepper to taste
- 2 tablespoons olive oil or butter

For the Red Wine Reduction:

- 1 cup red wine (such as Merlot or Cabernet Sauvignon)
- 1/2 cup beef or venison stock
- 2 tablespoons unsalted butter
- 1 shallot, finely chopped
- 2 cloves garlic, minced
- 1 tablespoon fresh thyme leaves
- Salt and pepper to taste

Instructions:

1. Season the Cervena venison steaks generously with salt and pepper on both sides.
2. Heat the olive oil or butter in a large skillet over medium-high heat.
3. Once hot, add the venison steaks to the skillet. Sear the steaks for 2-3 minutes on each side, or until they are browned on the outside but still pink in the center (for medium-rare). Adjust cooking time according to your desired level of doneness. Remove the steaks from the skillet and let them rest on a plate while you prepare the sauce.
4. In the same skillet, add the chopped shallot and minced garlic. Sauté for 1-2 minutes until softened and fragrant.
5. Pour the red wine into the skillet and bring it to a simmer. Let it cook for 2-3 minutes to reduce slightly.
6. Add the beef or venison stock to the skillet, along with the fresh thyme leaves. Stir to combine and let the sauce simmer for another 2-3 minutes to further reduce and thicken.

7. Stir in the unsalted butter until melted and incorporated into the sauce. Season the red wine reduction with salt and pepper to taste.
8. Return the seared Cervena venison steaks to the skillet, coating them with the red wine reduction. Let them heat through for 1-2 minutes.
9. Serve the Cervena steaks with red wine reduction immediately, spooning extra sauce over the top if desired.

Enjoy this elegant and flavorful dish of Cervena steak with red wine reduction, perfect for a special dinner occasion!

Hangi Pizza - Pizza with Hangi Meat and Vegetables

Ingredients:

For the Pizza Dough:

- 2 1/4 teaspoons (1 packet) active dry yeast
- 1 cup warm water
- 2 1/2 cups all-purpose flour
- 1 teaspoon salt
- 1 tablespoon olive oil

For the Hangi Toppings:

- Leftover hangi meat (such as chicken, pork, lamb, or beef), shredded or diced
- Leftover hangi vegetables (such as kumara, potatoes, pumpkin, carrots), diced
- 1 onion, thinly sliced
- 1 cup shredded mozzarella cheese
- 1/2 cup barbecue sauce or tomato sauce
- Fresh herbs (such as parsley or coriander), chopped, for garnish
- Salt and pepper to taste

Instructions:

1. Preheat your oven to 475°F (245°C). If you have a pizza stone, place it in the oven to preheat as well.
2. In a small bowl, dissolve the yeast in warm water and let it sit for about 5 minutes, until frothy.
3. In a large mixing bowl, combine the flour and salt. Make a well in the center and pour in the yeast mixture and olive oil. Stir until a dough forms.
4. Turn the dough out onto a lightly floured surface and knead it for about 5 minutes, until it is smooth and elastic. Shape the dough into a ball.
5. Place the dough ball in a lightly oiled bowl, cover it with a clean kitchen towel, and let it rise in a warm place for about 1 hour, or until doubled in size.
6. Once the dough has risen, punch it down and divide it into two equal portions. Roll out each portion of dough into a circle, about 12 inches in diameter.

7. Transfer the rolled-out pizza dough to a lightly greased pizza pan or parchment paper.
8. Spread barbecue sauce or tomato sauce over the surface of the pizza dough.
9. Top the pizza with shredded hangi meat, diced hangi vegetables, and sliced onion. Season with salt and pepper to taste.
10. Sprinkle shredded mozzarella cheese over the top of the pizza.
11. Transfer the pizza to the preheated oven (on the pizza stone, if using) and bake for 12-15 minutes, or until the crust is golden brown and the cheese is bubbly and melted.
12. Remove the pizza from the oven and let it cool for a few minutes before slicing.
13. Garnish the hangi pizza with chopped fresh herbs, if desired, before serving.

Enjoy this delicious and unique hangi pizza, combining the flavors of traditional Māori hangi with the beloved Italian classic!

King Salmon Fillet with Lemon Dill Sauce

Ingredients:

For the King Salmon:

- 4 king salmon fillets (about 6-8 ounces each), skin on
- Salt and pepper to taste
- 2 tablespoons olive oil or melted butter
- Lemon wedges, for serving

For the Lemon Dill Sauce:

- 1/2 cup mayonnaise
- 2 tablespoons fresh lemon juice
- 1 tablespoon Dijon mustard
- 1 tablespoon chopped fresh dill (or 1 teaspoon dried dill)
- 1 clove garlic, minced
- Salt and pepper to taste

Instructions:

1. Preheat your oven to 400°F (200°C). Line a baking sheet with parchment paper or foil.
2. Pat the king salmon fillets dry with paper towels and season them generously with salt and pepper on both sides.
3. Heat the olive oil or melted butter in a large oven-proof skillet over medium-high heat.
4. Once hot, add the salmon fillets to the skillet, skin side down. Sear the fillets for 2-3 minutes, until the skin is crispy and golden brown.
5. Carefully flip the salmon fillets over using a spatula. Transfer the skillet to the preheated oven and bake the salmon for 6-8 minutes, or until it is cooked through and flakes easily with a fork.
6. While the salmon is baking, prepare the lemon dill sauce. In a small bowl, whisk together the mayonnaise, fresh lemon juice, Dijon mustard, chopped fresh dill, minced garlic, salt, and pepper until smooth and well combined. Adjust seasoning to taste.

7. Once the salmon is cooked, remove it from the oven and let it rest for a few minutes.
8. Serve the king salmon fillets hot, drizzled with the lemon dill sauce. Garnish with additional fresh dill and lemon wedges on the side.
9. Enjoy your delicious king salmon fillets with lemon dill sauce as a main course, paired with your favorite sides such as roasted vegetables, rice, or a fresh salad.

This dish is perfect for a special dinner occasion or a weeknight treat, impressing with its vibrant flavors and elegant presentation!

New Zealand Sausages with Onion Gravy

Ingredients:

For the Sausages:

- 8-10 New Zealand-style sausages (such as beef, pork, or lamb)
- 2 tablespoons olive oil

For the Onion Gravy:

- 2 large onions, thinly sliced
- 2 tablespoons butter
- 2 tablespoons all-purpose flour
- 2 cups beef or vegetable broth
- 1 tablespoon Worcestershire sauce
- Salt and pepper to taste

Instructions:

1. Heat the olive oil in a large skillet over medium heat. Add the sausages to the skillet and cook them, turning occasionally, until they are browned on all sides and cooked through, about 10-15 minutes. Remove the sausages from the skillet and set them aside.
2. In the same skillet, melt the butter over medium heat. Add the sliced onions and cook, stirring occasionally, until they are soft and caramelized, about 15-20 minutes.
3. Sprinkle the flour over the caramelized onions and stir to coat evenly. Cook for another 1-2 minutes to cook off the raw flour taste.
4. Slowly pour in the beef or vegetable broth, stirring constantly, until the mixture thickens and becomes a gravy-like consistency. Add the Worcestershire sauce and season with salt and pepper to taste.
5. Return the cooked sausages to the skillet, coating them with the onion gravy. Let them heat through for another 2-3 minutes.
6. Serve the New Zealand sausages with onion gravy hot, accompanied by mashed potatoes, steamed vegetables, or crusty bread, if desired.

Enjoy this delicious and comforting dish of New Zealand sausages with onion gravy, perfect for a cozy dinner with family and friends!

Blue Cod and Paua (Abalone) Pie

Ingredients:

For the Pie Filling:

- 500g blue cod fillets, cut into bite-sized pieces
- 200g fresh or cooked paua (abalone), thinly sliced
- 1 onion, finely chopped
- 2 cloves garlic, minced
- 2 tablespoons butter
- 2 tablespoons all-purpose flour
- 1 cup seafood or fish stock
- 1/2 cup cream or milk
- 1/4 cup chopped fresh parsley
- Salt and pepper to taste

For the Pie Crust:

- 2 sheets of store-bought puff pastry, thawed
- 1 egg, beaten (for egg wash)

Instructions:

1. Preheat your oven to 375°F (190°C). Grease a pie dish or baking dish with butter or oil.
2. In a large skillet or frying pan, melt the butter over medium heat. Add the chopped onion and minced garlic, and sauté until softened and fragrant, about 2-3 minutes.
3. Add the blue cod pieces and sliced paua to the skillet. Cook for another 3-4 minutes, until the seafood is partially cooked. Remove the seafood from the skillet and set aside.
4. In the same skillet, sprinkle the flour over the melted butter and onion mixture. Stir to combine and cook for 1-2 minutes to form a roux.
5. Slowly pour in the seafood or fish stock, stirring constantly, until the mixture thickens and becomes a smooth sauce.

6. Stir in the cream or milk, chopped fresh parsley, and season with salt and pepper to taste. Cook for another 2-3 minutes, until the sauce is thickened and creamy.
7. Return the cooked blue cod and paua to the skillet, stirring to coat them with the sauce. Remove from heat.
8. Roll out one sheet of puff pastry and use it to line the bottom of the greased pie dish. Trim any excess pastry hanging over the edges.
9. Pour the seafood filling into the pie dish, spreading it out evenly.
10. Roll out the second sheet of puff pastry and place it over the top of the filling. Press the edges of the top and bottom crusts together to seal, then crimp the edges with a fork.
11. Brush the top of the pie with beaten egg for a golden finish.
12. Use a sharp knife to make a few small slits in the top crust to allow steam to escape during baking.
13. Place the pie in the preheated oven and bake for 30-35 minutes, or until the crust is golden brown and crispy.
14. Remove the blue cod and paua pie from the oven and let it cool for a few minutes before slicing and serving.

Enjoy this delicious and flavorful blue cod and paua pie as a special treat, perfect for a dinner party or gathering with friends and family!

Mussel Fritter Wrap with Lettuce and Tartare Sauce

Ingredients:

For the Mussel Fritters:

- 500g fresh green-lipped mussels, cleaned and debearded
- 1 cup all-purpose flour
- 1 teaspoon baking powder
- 1/2 teaspoon salt
- 1/4 teaspoon black pepper
- 1/2 cup milk
- 2 eggs, lightly beaten
- 2 tablespoons chopped fresh parsley
- Vegetable oil for frying

For the Tartare Sauce:

- 1/2 cup mayonnaise
- 2 tablespoons chopped gherkins or pickles
- 1 tablespoon capers, chopped
- 1 tablespoon lemon juice
- 1 tablespoon chopped fresh parsley
- Salt and pepper to taste

For the Wraps:

- Large flour tortillas or wraps
- Lettuce leaves, washed and dried

Instructions:

1. Start by making the tartare sauce. In a small bowl, mix together the mayonnaise, chopped gherkins or pickles, chopped capers, lemon juice, chopped parsley, salt, and pepper. Stir until well combined. Cover and refrigerate until ready to use.
2. Prepare the mussel fritters. In a large bowl, sift together the all-purpose flour, baking powder, salt, and black pepper.

3. In a separate bowl, whisk together the milk and beaten eggs. Gradually pour the wet ingredients into the dry ingredients, stirring until a smooth batter forms.
4. Add the cleaned and debearded mussels to the batter, along with the chopped fresh parsley. Stir gently to coat the mussels evenly with the batter.
5. Heat vegetable oil in a large skillet or frying pan over medium-high heat. Drop spoonfuls of the mussel batter into the hot oil, flattening them slightly with the back of the spoon to form fritters. Cook for 2-3 minutes on each side, or until golden brown and cooked through. Remove the fritters from the skillet and drain on paper towels.
6. To assemble the wraps, place a large flour tortilla or wrap on a clean work surface. Arrange lettuce leaves in the center of the tortilla.
7. Place a few mussel fritters on top of the lettuce leaves.
8. Spoon tartare sauce over the fritters.
9. Fold the sides of the tortilla over the filling, then roll it up tightly to form a wrap.
10. Repeat with the remaining tortillas and filling ingredients.
11. Serve the mussel fritter wraps immediately, or wrap them in parchment paper or foil for easy transport.

Enjoy these delicious and flavorful mussel fritter wraps with lettuce and tartare sauce for a tasty seafood meal!

New Zealand Mince Pie with Tomato Sauce

Ingredients:

For the Mince Filling:

- 500g minced beef or lamb
- 1 onion, finely chopped
- 2 cloves garlic, minced
- 1 carrot, grated
- 1 celery stalk, finely chopped
- 1 tablespoon tomato paste
- 1 tablespoon Worcestershire sauce
- 1 teaspoon dried mixed herbs (such as thyme, oregano, and rosemary)
- Salt and pepper to taste
- 1 cup beef or vegetable stock
- 2 tablespoons olive oil

For the Pastry:

- Store-bought shortcrust pastry or puff pastry (enough for 2 pie crusts)
- 1 egg, beaten (for egg wash)

For Serving:

- Tomato sauce (ketchup)

Instructions:

1. Preheat your oven to 200°C (400°F).
2. Heat olive oil in a large skillet or frying pan over medium heat. Add the chopped onion and minced garlic and cook until softened, about 3-4 minutes.
3. Add the minced beef or lamb to the skillet and cook until browned, breaking it up with a spoon as it cooks.
4. Stir in the grated carrot, chopped celery, tomato paste, Worcestershire sauce, dried mixed herbs, salt, and pepper. Cook for another 2-3 minutes to allow the flavors to meld.

5. Pour in the beef or vegetable stock and simmer for 15-20 minutes, or until the liquid has reduced and the mince filling has thickened. Remove from heat and let it cool slightly.
6. While the mince filling is cooling, prepare the pastry. Roll out the shortcrust pastry or puff pastry on a lightly floured surface to about 3-5mm thickness. Cut out circles or squares large enough to line your pie dishes.
7. Line your pie dishes with the pastry, leaving some excess hanging over the edges.
8. Spoon the cooled mince filling into the pastry-lined pie dishes.
9. Roll out the remaining pastry to make lids for the pies. Place the pastry lids over the filling and press the edges to seal. Trim any excess pastry with a knife and crimp the edges with a fork.
10. Brush the tops of the pies with beaten egg for a golden finish.
11. Use a sharp knife to make a few small slits in the top crust to allow steam to escape during baking.
12. Place the pies on a baking sheet and bake in the preheated oven for 20-25 minutes, or until the pastry is golden brown and crispy.
13. Remove the pies from the oven and let them cool for a few minutes before serving.
14. Serve the New Zealand mince pies with tomato sauce (ketchup) on the side for dipping.

Enjoy these delicious and comforting mince pies, a beloved staple of New Zealand cuisine!

Tuatua (Native New Zealand Clam) Soup

Ingredients:

- 1 kg tuatua clams (or substitute with other small clams)
- 2 tablespoons butter or olive oil
- 1 onion, finely chopped
- 2 cloves garlic, minced
- 2 medium potatoes, peeled and diced
- 2 carrots, peeled and diced
- 4 cups vegetable or seafood broth
- 1 cup coconut milk
- 1 teaspoon ground turmeric
- Salt and pepper to taste
- Fresh parsley or cilantro for garnish
- Lemon wedges for serving

Instructions:

1. Clean and Prepare the Tuatua Clams:
   - Rinse the tuatua clams under cold water to remove any sand or debris. Discard any clams that are open and do not close when tapped lightly.
2. Cook the Clams:
   - In a large pot, melt the butter or heat the olive oil over medium heat.
   - Add the finely chopped onion and minced garlic to the pot. Cook until the onion is soft and translucent, about 5 minutes.
   - Add the cleaned tuatua clams to the pot and pour in the vegetable or seafood broth.
   - Cover the pot and simmer for 5-7 minutes, or until the clams have opened. Discard any clams that do not open.
3. Remove Clams and Strain Broth:
   - Use a slotted spoon to transfer the cooked clams to a bowl. Set aside.
   - Strain the broth through a fine-mesh sieve or cheesecloth to remove any sand or grit. Return the strained broth to the pot.
4. Add Vegetables and Seasonings:
   - Add the diced potatoes and carrots to the pot with the strained broth.
   - Season with ground turmeric, salt, and pepper to taste.
   - Bring the broth to a simmer and cook until the vegetables are tender, about 10-15 minutes.
5. Prepare the Clams:

- Once the clams are cool enough to handle, remove the meat from the shells and discard the shells. Set the clam meat aside.

6. Finish the Soup:
    - Stir in the coconut milk into the pot with the cooked vegetables and broth.
    - Add the reserved clam meat to the soup and heat through.
    - Taste and adjust seasoning if needed.
7. Serve:
    - Ladle the tuatua clam soup into bowls.
    - Garnish with fresh parsley or cilantro.
    - Serve hot with lemon wedges on the side for squeezing over the soup.

Enjoy this delicious tuatua clam soup as a comforting and flavorful dish, perfect for showcasing the unique flavors of New Zealand's native clams!

New Zealand Lamb Shanks with Rosemary and Garlic

Ingredients:

- 4 lamb shanks
- Salt and pepper to taste
- 2 tablespoons olive oil
- 1 onion, finely chopped
- 4 cloves garlic, minced
- 2 carrots, diced
- 2 celery stalks, diced
- 2 cups beef or vegetable broth
- 1 cup red wine (such as Merlot or Cabernet Sauvignon)
- 2 sprigs fresh rosemary
- 4 sprigs fresh thyme
- 2 bay leaves
- 2 tablespoons tomato paste
- 1 tablespoon Worcestershire sauce
- 1 tablespoon balsamic vinegar
- Mashed potatoes or crusty bread, for serving
- Chopped fresh parsley for garnish

Instructions:

1. Preheat the Oven:
    - Preheat your oven to 350°F (175°C).
2. Season the Lamb Shanks:
    - Season the lamb shanks generously with salt and pepper.
3. Brown the Lamb Shanks:
    - Heat the olive oil in a large oven-safe Dutch oven or deep skillet over medium-high heat.
    - Add the lamb shanks to the skillet and brown on all sides, about 4-5 minutes per side. Remove the browned lamb shanks from the skillet and set aside.
4. Cook the Aromatics:
    - In the same skillet, add the chopped onion, minced garlic, diced carrots, and diced celery. Cook, stirring occasionally, until the vegetables are softened, about 5 minutes.
5. Deglaze the Pan:

- Pour in the red wine and scrape up any browned bits from the bottom of the skillet with a wooden spoon. Let the wine simmer for 2-3 minutes to reduce slightly.

6. Add the Remaining Ingredients:
   - Return the browned lamb shanks to the skillet.
   - Add the beef or vegetable broth, fresh rosemary, fresh thyme, bay leaves, tomato paste, Worcestershire sauce, and balsamic vinegar to the skillet. Stir to combine.

7. Braise the Lamb Shanks:
   - Cover the skillet with a lid or aluminum foil and transfer it to the preheated oven.
   - Braise the lamb shanks in the oven for 2-3 hours, or until the meat is tender and falling off the bone. Check periodically and add more broth if needed to keep the shanks moist.

8. Serve:
   - Once the lamb shanks are cooked to perfection, remove them from the oven.
   - Serve the lamb shanks hot with mashed potatoes or crusty bread to soak up the delicious sauce.
   - Garnish with chopped fresh parsley before serving.

9. Enjoy:
   - Enjoy this flavorful New Zealand lamb shanks with rosemary and garlic dish, perfect for a cozy dinner or special occasion!

This dish pairs beautifully with a glass of red wine and makes for a memorable meal that will impress your family and friends.

Whitebait Omelette with Chives

Ingredients:

- 1 cup fresh whitebait
- 4 large eggs
- 2 tablespoons milk or cream
- Salt and pepper to taste
- 2 tablespoons butter or olive oil
- 2 tablespoons chopped fresh chives
- Lemon wedges for serving

Instructions:

1. Prepare the Whitebait:
   - Rinse the fresh whitebait under cold water and pat dry with paper towels. Remove any excess moisture.
2. Whisk the Eggs:
   - In a mixing bowl, whisk together the eggs, milk or cream, salt, and pepper until well combined. The milk or cream adds richness to the omelette.
3. Cook the Whitebait:
   - In a non-stick skillet, heat 1 tablespoon of butter or olive oil over medium-high heat.
   - Add the whitebait to the skillet and cook for 1-2 minutes, stirring gently, until the whitebait is just cooked through. Be careful not to overcook the whitebait, as it cooks quickly.
4. Make the Omelette:
   - Reduce the heat to medium-low. Pour the beaten eggs into the skillet with the whitebait.
   - As the eggs begin to set around the edges, use a spatula to gently lift the edges and tilt the skillet to allow the uncooked eggs to flow to the bottom.
5. Add Chives:
   - Sprinkle the chopped fresh chives evenly over the omelette while the top is still slightly runny.
6. Fold and Serve:
   - Once the eggs are set but still slightly moist on top, fold the omelette in half using a spatula.
   - Cook for another 1-2 minutes, or until the eggs are cooked to your desired doneness.
7. Serve:

- Slide the whitebait omelette onto a serving plate.
- Garnish with additional chopped chives if desired.
- Serve hot with lemon wedges on the side for squeezing over the omelette.
8. Enjoy:
    - Enjoy this delicious whitebait omelette with chives as a breakfast or brunch dish, accompanied by crusty bread or a side salad.

This simple yet flavorful omelette highlights the unique taste of New Zealand whitebait and is a beloved dish enjoyed by locals and visitors alike.

Taro Fries with Sweet Chili Sauce

Ingredients:

For the Taro Fries:

- 2 medium taro roots
- 2 tablespoons olive oil
- Salt to taste
- Optional: 1 teaspoon paprika or garlic powder for added flavor

For the Sweet Chili Sauce:

- 1/2 cup sweet chili sauce
- 2 tablespoons soy sauce
- 1 tablespoon rice vinegar
- 1 tablespoon lime juice
- 1 teaspoon minced garlic
- 1 teaspoon minced ginger
- Optional: Red pepper flakes for added heat

Instructions:

1. Prepare the Taro Fries:
    - Preheat your oven to 400°F (200°C).
    - Peel the taro roots and cut them into thin strips resembling French fries.
    - Place the taro fries in a large bowl and toss with olive oil until evenly coated. If desired, sprinkle with salt and optional seasonings such as paprika or garlic powder.
2. Bake the Taro Fries:
    - Arrange the taro fries in a single layer on a baking sheet lined with parchment paper.
    - Bake in the preheated oven for 25-30 minutes, flipping halfway through, or until the fries are golden brown and crispy.
3. Make the Sweet Chili Sauce:
    - In a small saucepan, combine the sweet chili sauce, soy sauce, rice vinegar, lime juice, minced garlic, and minced ginger.
    - Optional: Add red pepper flakes for added heat if desired.

    - Heat the sauce over medium heat, stirring occasionally, until heated through and slightly thickened. Remove from heat.
4. Serve:
    - Once the taro fries are cooked to perfection, remove them from the oven and transfer them to a serving plate.
    - Serve the taro fries hot with the sweet chili sauce on the side for dipping.
5. Enjoy:
    - Enjoy these crispy and flavorful taro fries with sweet chili sauce as a tasty appetizer or snack!

The natural sweetness and starchy texture of taro root make these fries a unique and satisfying alternative to traditional potato fries. Paired with the tangy and slightly spicy sweet chili sauce, they create a delicious flavor combination that is sure to be a hit with friends and family.

Kingfish Fillet with Mango Salsa

Ingredients:

For the Kingfish:

- 4 kingfish fillets
- Salt and pepper to taste
- 2 tablespoons olive oil
- 1 tablespoon lemon juice

For the Mango Salsa:

- 2 ripe mangoes, peeled, pitted, and diced
- 1/2 red onion, finely chopped
- 1 red bell pepper, diced
- 1 jalapeño pepper, seeded and minced (optional, for heat)
- 1/4 cup chopped fresh cilantro
- Juice of 1 lime
- Salt and pepper to taste

Instructions:

1. Prepare the Kingfish:
    - Pat the kingfish fillets dry with paper towels and season them with salt and pepper on both sides.
    - In a bowl, combine the olive oil and lemon juice. Brush the mixture over the kingfish fillets, coating them evenly.
2. Grill or Pan-Sear the Kingfish:
    - Heat a grill or grill pan over medium-high heat. Alternatively, you can pan-sear the fillets in a skillet.
    - Grill or sear the kingfish fillets for about 3-4 minutes per side, or until cooked through and golden brown on the outside. Cooking time may vary depending on the thickness of the fillets.
3. Make the Mango Salsa:
    - In a separate bowl, combine the diced mangoes, chopped red onion, diced red bell pepper, minced jalapeño pepper (if using), and chopped fresh cilantro.
    - Squeeze the lime juice over the salsa and toss to combine.

- Season with salt and pepper to taste. Adjust the seasoning as needed.
4. Serve:
    - Once the kingfish fillets are cooked, transfer them to serving plates.
    - Spoon the mango salsa over the top of each fillet, allowing the vibrant colors and flavors to enhance the dish.
    - Garnish with additional cilantro leaves if desired.
5. Enjoy:
    - Serve the kingfish fillets with mango salsa immediately, accompanied by your favorite side dishes such as rice, quinoa, or roasted vegetables.

This kingfish fillet with mango salsa dish is perfect for a light and flavorful meal that's bursting with tropical goodness. It's ideal for entertaining guests or for a special dinner at home.

Kiwi Roast Chicken with Stuffing

Ingredients:

For the Roast Chicken:

- 1 whole chicken (about 4-5 pounds)
- Salt and pepper to taste
- 2 tablespoons olive oil or melted butter
- 1 lemon, quartered
- Fresh herbs such as rosemary, thyme, and parsley (optional)

For the Stuffing:

- 4 cups bread cubes (from stale bread)
- 2 tablespoons butter
- 1 onion, finely chopped
- 2 stalks celery, finely chopped
- 2 cloves garlic, minced
- 1 apple, peeled, cored, and diced
- 1/2 cup chopped walnuts or pecans (optional)
- 1/2 cup dried cranberries or raisins
- 1 teaspoon dried sage
- 1 teaspoon dried thyme
- 1/2 teaspoon dried rosemary
- Salt and pepper to taste
- 1-2 cups chicken broth or vegetable broth

Instructions:

1. Preheat the Oven:
    - Preheat your oven to 375°F (190°C).
2. Prepare the Chicken:
    - Remove the giblets from the cavity of the chicken, if included. Rinse the chicken under cold water and pat dry with paper towels.
    - Season the cavity of the chicken generously with salt and pepper. Stuff the cavity with lemon quarters and fresh herbs, if using.
    - Tie the legs together with kitchen twine and tuck the wing tips under the body of the chicken.

3. Prepare the Stuffing:
   - In a large skillet, melt the butter over medium heat. Add the chopped onion and celery, and cook until softened, about 5 minutes.
   - Add the minced garlic, diced apple, chopped nuts (if using), dried cranberries or raisins, dried sage, dried thyme, dried rosemary, salt, and pepper. Cook for an additional 2-3 minutes, until fragrant.
   - Remove the skillet from the heat and stir in the bread cubes until well combined. Gradually add chicken broth, stirring until the stuffing is moistened but not soggy.
4. Stuff the Chicken:
   - Spoon the prepared stuffing into the cavity of the chicken until it is filled. Do not pack the stuffing too tightly, as it needs room to expand during cooking.
   - Secure the opening of the cavity with toothpicks or skewers to prevent the stuffing from falling out during roasting.
5. Roast the Chicken:
   - Place the stuffed chicken in a roasting pan or baking dish. Drizzle the olive oil or melted butter over the surface of the chicken and rub it evenly.
   - Roast the chicken in the preheated oven for about 1.5 to 2 hours, or until the internal temperature reaches 165°F (75°C) when measured with a meat thermometer inserted into the thickest part of the thigh.
   - If the skin begins to brown too quickly, tent the chicken loosely with aluminum foil to prevent burning.
6. Rest and Serve:
   - Once the chicken is cooked through, remove it from the oven and let it rest for 10-15 minutes before carving.
   - Carve the roast chicken into serving portions and serve with the delicious stuffing alongside.
7. Enjoy:
   - Enjoy this flavorful and comforting Kiwi roast chicken with stuffing as a hearty main course for a special occasion or family dinner!

This Kiwi-inspired roast chicken with stuffing is sure to be a hit at your table, combining tender roast chicken with a savory and aromatic stuffing that's packed with delicious flavors.

New Zealand Green Lip Mussels in Garlic Butter Sauce

Ingredients:

- 2 pounds New Zealand green lip mussels, cleaned and debearded
- 4 tablespoons butter
- 4 cloves garlic, minced
- 1/4 cup white wine or chicken broth
- 1 tablespoon lemon juice
- 2 tablespoons chopped fresh parsley
- Salt and pepper to taste
- Crusty bread or French baguette, for serving

Instructions:

1. Prepare the Mussels:
   - Rinse the green lip mussels under cold water to remove any dirt or debris. Scrub the shells with a brush to clean them thoroughly. Remove the beards by pulling them gently towards the hinge of the shell. Discard any mussels that are open and do not close when tapped lightly.
2. Make the Garlic Butter Sauce:
   - In a large skillet or saucepan, melt the butter over medium heat.
   - Add the minced garlic to the skillet and cook for 1-2 minutes, stirring frequently, until fragrant.
3. Cook the Mussels:
   - Increase the heat to medium-high. Add the cleaned mussels to the skillet.
   - Pour in the white wine or chicken broth and lemon juice over the mussels.
   - Cover the skillet with a lid and cook for 5-7 minutes, or until the mussels have opened. Discard any mussels that do not open.
4. Season and Serve:
   - Once the mussels have opened, remove the skillet from the heat.
   - Season the mussels with salt and pepper to taste, and sprinkle chopped fresh parsley over the top.
5. Serve:
   - Transfer the cooked mussels and garlic butter sauce to a serving dish.
   - Serve the New Zealand green lip mussels hot, accompanied by crusty bread or French baguette slices for dipping into the flavorful sauce.
6. Enjoy:
   - Enjoy these succulent New Zealand green lip mussels in garlic butter sauce as a delicious appetizer or light meal!

This dish is perfect for seafood lovers and makes a delightful addition to any dinner party or gathering. The combination of tender mussels and fragrant garlic butter sauce is sure to impress your guests and tantalize your taste buds.

Crumbed Blue Cod Fillet with Tartare Sauce

Ingredients:

For the Crumbed Blue Cod:

- 4 blue cod fillets
- Salt and pepper to taste
- 1/2 cup all-purpose flour
- 2 eggs, beaten
- 1 cup breadcrumbs (panko or homemade)
- 2 tablespoons vegetable oil for frying

For the Tartare Sauce:

- 1/2 cup mayonnaise
- 2 tablespoons chopped dill pickles or gherkins
- 1 tablespoon capers, chopped
- 1 tablespoon fresh lemon juice
- 1 tablespoon chopped fresh parsley
- 1 teaspoon Dijon mustard
- Salt and pepper to taste

For Serving:

- Lemon wedges
- Fresh parsley for garnish

Instructions:

1. Prepare the Tartare Sauce:
    - In a small bowl, combine the mayonnaise, chopped dill pickles or gherkins, chopped capers, fresh lemon juice, chopped fresh parsley, and Dijon mustard. Stir until well combined.
    - Season the tartare sauce with salt and pepper to taste. Cover and refrigerate until ready to serve.
2. Prepare the Blue Cod Fillets:
    - Pat the blue cod fillets dry with paper towels and season them with salt and pepper.

- Set up a breading station with three shallow bowls: one with flour, one with beaten eggs, and one with breadcrumbs.
- Dredge each blue cod fillet in the flour, shaking off any excess. Dip it into the beaten eggs, allowing any excess to drip off, then coat it evenly with breadcrumbs, pressing gently to adhere.

3. Fry the Blue Cod Fillets:
   - Heat the vegetable oil in a large skillet over medium-high heat.
   - Carefully add the breaded blue cod fillets to the hot oil, working in batches if necessary to avoid overcrowding the skillet.
   - Fry the fillets for 3-4 minutes on each side, or until golden brown and crispy. The internal temperature of the fish should reach 145°F (63°C) to ensure it's cooked through.
   - Transfer the cooked blue cod fillets to a paper towel-lined plate to drain any excess oil.
4. Serve:
   - Serve the crumbed blue cod fillets hot, garnished with fresh parsley and lemon wedges on the side.
   - Serve the tartare sauce alongside the fish for dipping or drizzling.
5. Enjoy:
   - Enjoy this delicious crumbed blue cod fillet with tartare sauce as a main dish, accompanied by your favorite side dishes such as fries, salad, or steamed vegetables.

This dish is a popular choice in New Zealand and is loved for its crispy exterior, tender fish, and flavorful tartare sauce. It's perfect for a family dinner or a special occasion meal.

Venison Sausages with Onion Gravy and Mashed Potatoes

Ingredients:

For the Venison Sausages:

- 4-6 venison sausages
- 2 tablespoons olive oil

For the Onion Gravy:

- 2 large onions, thinly sliced
- 2 tablespoons butter
- 2 tablespoons all-purpose flour
- 2 cups beef or vegetable broth
- Salt and pepper to taste

For the Mashed Potatoes:

- 4 large potatoes, peeled and diced
- 1/4 cup butter
- 1/2 cup milk or cream
- Salt and pepper to taste

Optional Garnish:

- Chopped fresh parsley or chives

Instructions:

1. Cook the Venison Sausages:
   - Heat the olive oil in a large skillet over medium heat.
   - Add the venison sausages to the skillet and cook, turning occasionally, until browned on all sides and cooked through, about 10-12 minutes. Remove from the skillet and set aside.
2. Make the Onion Gravy:
   - In the same skillet, add the sliced onions and butter. Cook over medium heat, stirring occasionally, until the onions are soft and caramelized, about 10-15 minutes.

- Sprinkle the flour over the caramelized onions and stir to combine, cooking for an additional 1-2 minutes.
- Gradually pour in the beef or vegetable broth, stirring constantly to prevent lumps from forming.
- Bring the gravy to a simmer and cook until thickened, about 5-7 minutes. Season with salt and pepper to taste.

3. Prepare the Mashed Potatoes:
    - While the onion gravy is simmering, place the diced potatoes in a large pot and cover with water. Bring to a boil over high heat and cook until the potatoes are fork-tender, about 10-15 minutes.
    - Drain the cooked potatoes and return them to the pot.
    - Add the butter and milk or cream to the pot with the potatoes. Mash the potatoes using a potato masher until smooth and creamy. Season with salt and pepper to taste.
4. Serve:
    - Serve the venison sausages hot, accompanied by a generous serving of mashed potatoes.
    - Ladle the onion gravy over the sausages and mashed potatoes.
    - Garnish with chopped fresh parsley or chives, if desired.
5. Enjoy:
    - Enjoy this comforting and delicious dish of venison sausages with onion gravy and mashed potatoes, perfect for a cozy dinner on a chilly evening!

This dish is sure to warm you up and satisfy your appetite with its rich flavors and comforting textures. It's a favorite among venison lovers and is a great way to enjoy this flavorful meat in a classic and hearty meal.

Bluff Oyster Omelette

Ingredients:

- 6 fresh Bluff oysters, shucked
- 4 large eggs
- 1 tablespoon butter
- Salt and pepper to taste
- Chopped fresh parsley for garnish (optional)

Instructions:

1. Prepare the Bluff Oysters:
    - Rinse the Bluff oysters under cold water to remove any excess grit or shell fragments. Pat them dry with a paper towel.
2. Beat the Eggs:
    - In a mixing bowl, beat the eggs until well combined. Season with salt and pepper to taste.
3. Cook the Omelette:
    - Heat the butter in a non-stick skillet over medium heat until melted and foamy.
    - Pour the beaten eggs into the skillet, swirling to coat the bottom evenly.
    - Allow the eggs to cook undisturbed for a minute or two, until the edges begin to set.
4. Add the Bluff Oysters:
    - Arrange the shucked Bluff oysters evenly over one half of the omelette.
5. Fold the Omelette:
    - Using a spatula, carefully fold the other half of the omelette over the oysters to enclose them.
6. Finish Cooking:
    - Cook the omelette for another minute or two, until the eggs are fully set and the oysters are warmed through.
7. Serve:
    - Slide the Bluff oyster omelette onto a serving plate.
    - Garnish with chopped fresh parsley, if desired.
8. Enjoy:
    - Serve the Bluff oyster omelette hot, accompanied by your favorite side dishes such as toast, salad, or sautéed vegetables.

This Bluff oyster omelette is a simple yet elegant dish that highlights the unique flavor and texture of Bluff oysters. It's perfect for a leisurely breakfast, brunch, or light dinner, and is sure to impress your guests with its delicious taste.

Manuka Honey Glazed Duck Breast

Ingredients:

- 2 duck breasts
- Salt and pepper to taste
- 2 tablespoons Manuka honey
- 2 tablespoons soy sauce
- 1 tablespoon balsamic vinegar
- 2 cloves garlic, minced
- 1 teaspoon grated ginger
- 1 tablespoon olive oil
- Fresh parsley or green onions for garnish (optional)

Instructions:

1. Prepare the Duck Breasts:
    - Score the skin of the duck breasts in a crisscross pattern, being careful not to cut into the meat. This helps the fat render and the skin to crisp up during cooking.
    - Season both sides of the duck breasts generously with salt and pepper.
2. Make the Glaze:
    - In a small bowl, whisk together the Manuka honey, soy sauce, balsamic vinegar, minced garlic, and grated ginger until well combined.
3. Marinate the Duck Breasts:
    - Place the duck breasts in a shallow dish or resealable plastic bag. Pour the prepared glaze over the duck breasts, making sure they are evenly coated. Marinate in the refrigerator for at least 30 minutes, or up to 4 hours, to allow the flavors to meld.
4. Preheat the Oven:
    - Preheat your oven to 400°F (200°C).
5. Sear the Duck Breasts:
    - Heat the olive oil in an oven-safe skillet over medium-high heat.
    - Once the skillet is hot, add the duck breasts, skin-side down. Sear for 3-4 minutes, or until the skin is golden brown and crispy. Be careful as the fat may splatter.
    - Flip the duck breasts over and sear the other side for an additional 2 minutes.
6. Glaze and Roast:

- Brush the tops of the duck breasts with some of the remaining glaze from the marinade.
- Transfer the skillet to the preheated oven and roast for 8-10 minutes, or until the duck breasts reach your desired level of doneness. The internal temperature should register 130-135°F (55-57°C) for medium-rare or 140-145°F (60-63°C) for medium when measured with a meat thermometer inserted into the thickest part of the breast.

7. Rest and Serve:
    - Remove the duck breasts from the oven and let them rest for 5 minutes before slicing.
    - Slice the duck breasts thinly against the grain and arrange them on serving plates.
    - Drizzle any remaining glaze from the skillet over the sliced duck breasts.
8. Garnish and Enjoy:
    - Garnish with fresh parsley or sliced green onions, if desired.
    - Serve the Manuka honey glazed duck breast hot, accompanied by your favorite side dishes such as roasted vegetables or wild rice.

This Manuka honey glazed duck breast is a sophisticated and flavorful dish that's perfect for special occasions or romantic dinners. The combination of tender duck meat with the sweet and savory glaze is sure to impress your guests and elevate your meal to new heights.

www.ingramcontent.com/pod-product-compliance
Lightning Source LLC
LaVergne TN
LVHW062048070526
838201LV00080B/2200